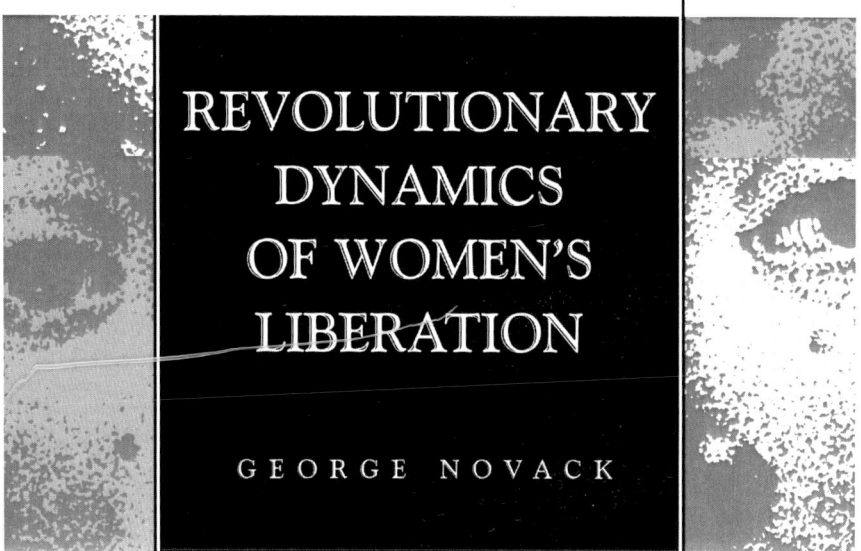

REVOLUTIONARY DYNAMICS OF WOMEN'S LIBERATION

GEORGE NOVACK

PATHFINDER
NEW YORK   LONDON   MONTREAL   SYDNEY

Copyright © 1969 by Pathfinder Press
All rights reserved

ISBN 978-0-87348-120-5
Library of Congress Control Number 2010930322
Manufactured in Canada

First edition, 1969
Tenth printing, 2026

This article was first published in the *Militant* on October 17, 1969.

COVER DESIGN: Eva Braiman

PATHFINDER
pathfinderpress.com
Email: pathfinder@pathfinderpress.com

Revolutionary dynamics of women's liberation

THE CURRENT FERMENT in society around the issue of women's liberation betokens a new and higher phase of a social struggle which has periodically erupted in the West for two hundred years. The slogan of female equality is democratic in character although full emancipation for women can be realized only through a socialist revolution. This demand asserts the legitimate right of one-half the human race to be placed on a par in all respects—legal, social, economic, educational—with the dominant male half.

This kind of demand is at odds with the patriarchal, feudal conception of woman's place in society, which was tersely formulated by John Milton, who fought for the right of divorce and had an enlightened attitude toward women for his time, in *Paradise Lost:*

> Man was made for God
> and woman was made for man.

The general struggle for political democracy and civil rights against the hierarchical institutions, customs and standards of the precapitalist past dates back to the 16th century. It began with the 80-year war to free the Netherlands from Spanish shackles, continued through the two English revolutions of the following century and the American and French revolutions of the last quarter of the eighteenth century, and terminated in the American civil war.

As these mobilizations for democratic objectives unfolded, the ruling powers were compelled to take cognizance of the most insistent needs of the masses. The big bourgeoisie, which was the principal beneficiary of these upheavals, was disposed to short-change the claims of the plebeians. But the exigencies of overcoming their feudal foes, consolidating their supremacy, and maintaining social and political stability prevented them from totally denying the demands from the lower orders and enabled the latter to make considerable advances over feudal times in their freedoms.

'The rights of the people'
The appeal made by the bourgeois radicals to "the rights of the people" against the privileges and prerogatives of the old regime had tremendous dynamism. This abstract slogan, which inspired the democratic forces, became a seedbed for the sprouting of specific demands articulating the urgent needs of diverse contingents of the oppressed. These passed from the peasants, wage workers, slaves and subject nationalities to the religiously persecuted, racially discriminated, pariahs and paupers, the aged, the sick and disabled, criminals and prisoners, the insane, and the young. As the democratic movement and its ideals spread through bourgeois society, each of these downtrodden groups found defenders and evangels who strove to secure redress of their

grievances and betterment of their situations.

The first cries for women's liberation resounded in this historical setting. Whenever the rest of society was shaken up and set into motion during the bourgeois era, what was then termed "the distaff side" of the population was sooner or later stirred up, and calls for reforms in their subordinate status came from militant women as well as sympathetic males.

It is noteworthy that, in contrast to protests by isolated individuals, sustained movements for women's rights emerged rather late in the upswing of bourgeois society. This tardiness was in itself an index to the extent of the oppression and submissiveness from which women suffered. They were slow to rouse themselves, organize, and act in a concerted and self-confident manner.

The Levellers

Although the women of Holland and Great Britain played active and prominent parts in many of the most dramatic developments of the Dutch and English revolutions, they were kept in the rear and assumed minimal roles in political affairs. Their place was still in the home, not in public life. The Levellers, for example, who were the most vigorous exponents of democracy in the British civil war and whose leaders displayed high regard for the capacities of their women adherents, did not request any share in government for them, any more than they proposed to extend the franchise to "servants," as the wage workers were then designated.

The American colonists could not have settled and cultivated the land without the skills and strength of the pioneer women, nor could they have waged their seven-year war of independence successfully without the efforts and sacrifices of their wives, sisters and mothers. In 1777, at the start of armed conflict, Abigail Adams, wife of John Adams, wrote her husband: "In the new code of laws which I suppose it will be necessary for you to make, I desire you should remember the ladies and be more generous and favorable to them than your ancestors. Do not put such unlimited power into the hands of the husbands. Remember, all men would be tyrants if they could. If particular care and attention is not paid to the ladies, we are determined to foment a rebellion, and will not hold ourselves bound by any laws in which we had no voice or representation."

Her half-jocular plea was not acted upon. When the U.S. republic was founded, women received little more political recognition than did the black slaves.

French revolution

On the other side of the Atlantic, the materialist philosopher Condorcet, under prodding from his wife, was one of the first, and very few, male heralds of the French revolution to propose giving women certain political rights. In 1790 he declared that "either no member of the human race has true rights or all have the same." But his attitude was exceptional among the spokesmen of the time.

The 8,000 working-class women who marched on Versailles in October 1789 were instrumental in breaking the royal power, and the women of Paris played a decisive role in all the great days which accelerated the revolution. Yet that epoch-making charter of bourgeois democracy, the Declaration of the Rights of Man and the Citizen, adopted in 1789, did not provide any special civil rights for the women of France.

Four years after this declaration was proclaimed, Olympe de Gouges, the daughter of a butcher who was one of the first champions of her sex to write on politics, published a Declaration of the Rights of Women. It contained these memorable lines: "Women are born free and equal to men in their rights. . . . Women have the right to go to the scaffold; they should also have the right to ascend the tribune. . . . Women, arise!"

However, many leaders of the first women's organizations were guillotined and imprisoned and the Convention voted to dissolve and prohibit all the women's clubs that had sprung up under the impetus of the revolution. Whereas divorce was authorized in 1792, the Napoleonic Code of 1804 placed the wife under strict subordination to the husband.

England

Despite figures like Mary Wollstonecraft, a radical critic of many spheres of social life, who issued one of the earliest challenges to male supremacy in her *Vindication of the Rights of Women,* published in 1792, public agitation for women's rights in the English-speaking countries does not go back much further than 150 years ago. Interest in the question arose in England soon after the passage of the Reform Bill of 1832, which somewhat liberalized the franchise.

Industrialization

So long as the rural family with its cottage industry remained intact, the plight of women attracted little public attention. This changed when large-scale industry pulled increasing numbers of women and small children into the mills and shops, where they were pitilessly ground down. Their severance from the home and entry into social production singled out the sex for the first time as a force apart from the family. Thanks to the propaganda of the proletarian Chartists as well as middle-class reformers and writers, the problem of working women came to the fore between 1832 and 1850.

During this same period, the feminist movement in the United States was stimulated by the visit in 1820 of the Scottish reformer Frances Wright. She contended against conventional prejudices on the proper position of women and called for an end to their social degradation. The struggle for women's equality before the civil war became closely associated with the other reform crusades of the time, and especially with antislavery agitation. The matter of the priorities to be accorded the two issues generated dissension among the Abolitionists.

The first Women's Rights Convention was held in Seneca Falls, New York, in 1848, the year that saw the publication of the *Communist Manifesto*. It adopted a Declaration of Sentiments, patterned after the Declaration of Independence, which was somewhat ecclesiastical and middle-class in flavor. But the document deserves extensive quotation for its forceful indictment of the "long train of abuses" inflicted upon American women and the determination expressed by the most defiant defenders of their cause over a century ago:

Declaration of Sentiments

"The history of mankind is a history of repeated injuries and usurpations on the part of men toward woman, having in direct object the establishment of an absolute tyranny over her. To prove this, let facts be submitted to a candid world.

"He has never permitted her to exercise her inalienable

right to elective franchise.

"He has compelled her to submit to laws, in the formation of which she had no voice.

"He has withheld from her rights which are given to the most ignorant and degraded men—both natives and foreigners.

"Having deprived her of this first right of a citizen, the elective franchise, thereby leaving her without representation in the halls of legislation, he has oppressed her on all sides.

"He has made her, if married, in the eye of the law, civilly dead.

"He has taken from her all right in property, even to the wages she earns.

"He has made her, morally, an irresponsible being, as she can commit many crimes with impunity, provided they be done in the presence of her husband. In the covenant of marriage, she is compelled to promise obedience to her husband, he becoming to all intents and purposes, her master—the law giving him power to deprive her of her liberty, and to administer chastisement.

"He has so framed the laws of divorce, as to what shall be the proper causes, and, in case of separation, to whom the guardianship of the children shall be given, as to be wholly regardless of the happiness of women—the law in all cases going upon a false supposition of the supremacy of men, and giving all power into his hands.

"After depriving her of all rights as a married woman, if single, and the owner of property, he has taxed her to support a government which recognises her only when her property can be made profitable to it.

"He has monopolised nearly all the profitable employments, and from those she is permitted to follow she receives but a scanty remuneration. He closes against her all the avenues of wealth and distinction which he considers most honourable to himself. As a teacher of theology, medicine, or law, she is not known.

"He has denied her the facilities for obtaining a thorough education, all colleges being closed against her.

"He allows her in church, as well as state, but a subordinate position, claiming Apostolic authority for her exclusion from the ministry, and, with some exceptions, from any public participation in the affairs of the church.

"He has created a false public sentiment by giving to the world a different code of morals for men and women, by which moral delinquencies which exclude women from society are not only tolerated, but deemed of little account in man.

"He has usurped the prerogative of Jehovah himself, claiming it as his right to assign for her a sphere of action, when that belongs to her conscience and to her God.

"He has endeavoured, in every way that he could, to destroy her confidence in her own powers, to lessen her self-respect, and to make her willing to lead a dependent and abject life.

"Now, in view of this entire disfranchisement of one-half the people of this country, their social and religious degradation; in view of the unjust laws above mentioned, and because women do feel themselves aggrieved, oppressed, and fraudulently deprived of their most sacred rights, we insist that they have immediate admission to all the rights and privileges which belong to them as citizens of the United States.

"In entering upon the great work before us, we anticipate

no small amount of misconception, misrepresentation, and ridicule; but we shall use every instrumentality within our power to effect our object. We shall employ agents, circulate tracts, petition the State and National legislatures, and endeavor to enlist the pulpit and press in our behalf. We hope this Convention will be followed by a series of Conventions embracing every part of the country."

Freed slaves but not women
This initial nationwide campaign won some minor reforms for women before it had to be suspended at the outbreak of the civil war. The agitation for women's rights was rekindled by the palpable inequity of the Fourteenth Amendment of 1866, which granted voting rights to the freed slaves but not to women. The Northern men of money in charge of the Republican Party justified this discrimination because they could make use of black votes to beat the Democratic Party in the South but saw no political purpose in giving the franchise to the other sex.

It took over a hundred years of persistent endeavor by small bands of suffragists to break down the barriers, state by state, and finally force through the Nineteenth Amendment which, in 1920, legalized women's right to vote in national elections.

Civil rights
The gains in civil rights made by women in the most favored of capitalist nations indicate that the overcoming of the grosser disabilities inherited from patriarchal feudalism was one of the most difficult jobs encountered by the bourgeois movement of democratization. The obdurate resistance to their removal testifies both to their deep

roots in class society and to the conservatism of the upper classes, even in the most progressive periods of bourgeois development. They fear any tendencies which threaten to weaken the social supports of private property and profiteering upon which their system rests.

Male prejudice, family custom, religious beliefs and all the other baggage of the patriarchal past would not have deterred the capitalist class from equalizing the situation of American women much faster and further than they have done had it been in their interest to do so. But the exploiters have failed to promote the emancipation of women beyond its present limits for the same reasons that Afro-Americans have been held down and held back. More freedom for women would have been too costly and cut into the profit-making which is the be-all and end-all of the capitalist system.

Male predominance and female subordination is a permanent fixture in bourgeois society because this relation of inequality is an integral component of the mechanism of capitalist exploitation. Women are oppressed both within society as a whole and within the family. The fountainhead of that double degradation is their economic dependence upon the male wage-earner who is the initial recipient and disburser of the household income. If she does not have an outside job, the woman as daughter, sister, wife, mother and homebody relies for her ration upon the husband, father, and brother, who are in turn dependent upon the employer who buys their labor power.

Cheap labor power
In the second place, capitalists require not only cheap but constantly renewed supplies of labor power, which must

primarily come from the younger generation. Women have the prime responsibility for raising children. Their unpaid or poorly recompensed labors in the family household serve to lower the costs of reproducing and renewing the labor force.

These costs would be much higher if the capitalist regime had to take over the multiple services provided gratis or at minimal expenditure by the family setup and the domestic drudgery of married women. The socialization of such services would have to be paid for by taxation, which would in part fall upon the capitalists. This shift would increase the cost of the most vital factor of production, the work force which creates value, and reduce whatever advantage accrues to the national capitalist class in that respect.

Third, where women work in large numbers in industry, trade, offices, schools and the professions, discrimination against them is directly profitable to the employers. Degradation and domesticity keep them in the category of lower-paid labor. The capitalists always benefit from maintaining national, racial and sexual differentials in income and status among the work force. The working class as a whole would be a far more homogeneous and formidable antagonist if all discriminations and divisions within it were eliminated.

Fourth, women are a detachment of the reserve army of labor required by the capitalists during periods of labor shortage. This supply can be impounded or tapped according to the fluctuating rate of the accumulation of capital. During wartime, women can be mustered out of the household and drawn into the productive processes, as was done during the first and second world wars. Then, with the end of hostilities, they can be sent back to the family hearth, there to be kept in storage until capital needs to recall them again. The family home is a depot where surplus labor is deposited and kept in mothballs at least expense to the profiteers.

Prime targets

Fifth, females of all ages are the prime target of the advertising hucksters who must induce them, by fair means or foul, to purchase all kinds of commodities, useful and useless, from gadgets to cosmetics. In this con-game even the appliances which are supposed to relieve and lighten household toil become devices for fastening the family to the credit companies.

Social as well as economic reasons lead the possessing classes to shore up the cult of the family. The ordinary urban family with the male at its head acts as a stabilizing and conservatizing agency in an otherwise unsettled world. It is a corral where the domestic servant works for the master in the kitchen, nursery and dining room. Though the family nest may often provide the sole sanctuary from the buffetings and harassments of a cruel outside environment, it fosters immersion in purely private concerns, narrowness of outlook and exclusiveness among its members. Here attempts are made to tame, discipline and conservatize adolescents. All sorts of backwardness, from religion to racism, are nurtured within its walls.

These ever-present factors are more potent than long-standing prejudice in preventing the capitalist regime from giving women the freedom they desire. The rulers can under duress bestow upon women the same formal juridical, political and constitutional rights that men possess: the right to own and dispose of property, the right to vote and hold office, and the right to divorce, although these rights may be curtailed in practice. They can even be pressed to legalize birth control and abortion.

Bourgeois reforms

But just as the bourgeois revolution transformed the Southern chattel slaves into impoverished landless freedmen and then returned them to new forms of bondage, so bourgeois reforms have allowed women to escape from being a complete chattel of the male master and become a "free individual" in the bourgeois sense. What they have not done is to release women from the grip of the men and give them equality in the decisive spheres of social life.

The exploitative structure of their system sets limits on the scope of the freedoms the monopolists can grant to any segment of the oppressed. Just as the American capitalists have failed to give equality to the blacks a hundred years after the Emancipation Proclamation, so they have not truly emancipated women. They cannot make good on their promises of "liberty for all" because they lack the material incentives and class impulsions to do so.

Socialist revolution

It will take a thoroughgoing reorganization of the entire social setup from the economic foundations up to and including family relations before women can eradicate the causes of their inferior status and the evils flowing from it. In order to accomplish that, a socialist revolution, which will transfer state power and the ownership of the means of production from the monopolists to the majority of the people, must be carried through.

These are the lessons to be learned from the disappointing results of the democratic epoch in improving the position of the female sex and from examining the actual role of women, and especially working-class women, in the functioning of American capitalism today.

Permanent revolution

These conclusions likewise correspond with the tenets of the permanent revolution, which were projected by Marx and Engels in 1850 and elaborated by Leon Trotsky in the light of 20th century conditions. This theory affirms that, whereas the bourgeoisie could be a progressive and at times a revolutionizing force during the expansion of capitalism, this class has become more and more conservative and counterrevolutionary in the period of its decline and death agony.

Trotsky originally applied this proposition to the political role of the bourgeoisie in backward regions like Russia and the colonial world, which had not yet experienced a bourgeois-democratic revolution. As a Marxist, he took for granted the elementary premise of the socialist movement that the imperialist plutocracy of the industrial metropolises was utterly reactionary and had to be overthrown.

However, the historical-sociological generalization he made holds good not only for retarded countries which had not been democratized but also for those advanced capitalisms whose bourgeois revolutions defaulted in consummating their democratic assignments, as all of them did in one or another respect. Though our war of independence and civil war had many revolutionary accomplishments to their credit, they failed to make blacks equal with whites and women with men.

What has happened in the century since 1865 has served to aggravate both problems. Consequently, these unsolved tasks of the democratic era have been transmitted for solution to the next stage of revolutionary advancement in this country, which is centered around the struggle for socialism. The American revolution now in the making is called upon by the course of our national development to do two sets of jobs at one and the same time. It must tackle the unfinished business left over from the preceding revolutions, such as equality for blacks and women, together with the tasks connected with the construction of socialism. This simultaneous combination of missions belonging to successive stages of historical progress is characteristic of the age of permanent revolution we are living through.

Marxist interpretation

Some participants in the women's liberation ranks approach the intolerable predicament of their sex in a highly personalized and unpolitical way. They seek relief and release through some sort of psychological readjustment, antimale attitudes, or by gathering together in small utopian communes. These reactions are understandable in the first flush of revulsion against family domination and male chauvinism and in the desire to cast off the yoke of servitude without delay.

Indignation against injustice is a mighty motive force in the individual and in society. But bitter hatred for what is detestable has to be enlightened and guided by scientific understanding in order to become politically useful and socially effective. Rational inquiry into the underlying causes of the age-long oppression of women is indispensable for working out the best ways and means of attacking and abolishing it.

The Marxist explanation for the subjugation of women is based upon recognition of the fact that private ownership of the means of production, plus the right of property inheritance, was the prime condition for woman's downfall. This began at the dawn of class society and has provided the foundation and framework of her servitude throughout civilization. It persists today in the most developed countries because property and power are monopolized by the capitalist rulers.

What conclusions are to be drawn from these fundamental truths? First, that women cannot find freedom and independence or develop their capacities as a sex or as individuals within the confines of the most liberal capitalism. A liberal bourgeois attitude toward women involves no more than lengthening the chain which remains riveted to the stake of private property and the evils of the family, marital and sexual customs derived from it.

It also signifies that women cannot liberate themselves unless the socio-economic basis of male and capitalist supremacy is destroyed. A democratic workers' regime and the collective ownership of the means of production are required for any fundamental and beneficent transformation of the relations between men and women, husbands and wives, parents and children.

It further signifies that the exploited of both sexes must make common cause in getting rid of the capitalist class structure behind their deprivations.

Finally, it signifies that there can be no socialist movement and no socialism without the participation of women on an equal footing with men in all spheres of activity and without conscious counteraction against the habits of male chauvinism.

Total liberation

If the demand for woman's equality is democratic, the call for her total liberation can only be socialistic. The relations between capitalism and the struggle for democracy have undergone a dialectical reversal in the 20th century. During its confrontations with the feudalists, the progressive big and little bourgeoisie promoted democratic rights and institutions. Now, as imperialistic capitalism holds sway, the monopolists and militarists have become the deadliest enemies of democracy. They deny the elementary right of self-determination to other nationalities abroad and at home. They no longer safeguard and extend the previously acquired rights of the American people but imperil and chip away at them. Any large-scale effort to broaden democratic liberties must be directed against the repressive rule of the rich.

Under present conditions, the struggle for the expansion of freedom on any front and for any sector of the population cannot be separated from the anticapitalist movement of the workers, black and white. Only a socialist revolution can create the conditions for eliminating social inequalities of all types. Not least among these are the subjugation of women and the antagonisms between the sexes fostered by the alienations of a competitive capitalist environment.

Abominable treatment

The emergence of a new stage in the fight for women's liberation confronts revolutionary Marxists with a challenge and a responsibility. From its birth, the socialist movement has been acutely sensitive to the abominable treatment of the female sex in class society and has sought to find out its causes and combat its effects. Such utopian thinkers of the early 19th century as Saint-Simon, Fourier, and Owen were brilliant pioneers in this field. The scientific socialists who came after them have exposed the fraud of formal bourgeois equality between the sexes as well as between the contending classes. They have worked to reduce and remove the disabilities endured by women and, above all, to point and lead the way to their full emancipation.

Women have been one of the major forces in all the socialist revolutions of our time. The Russian Revolution and its sequels in Yugoslavia, China, Vietnam and Cuba have, whatever their deficiencies, introduced tremendous improvements in the lives of the terribly trampled upon women of these countries, raised their dignity and opened new vistas of opportunity and achievement to them.

Women abolitionists

All the earlier efforts to enlarge women's rights in our own country have been connected with broader movements of social protest. The pre-civil-war agitation was part of the upsurge against slavery. "It was in the abolition movement that women first learned to organize, to hold public meetings, to conduct petition campaigns," writes Eleanor Flexner. "As abolitionists they first won the right to speak in public, and began to evolve a philosophy of their place in society and of their basic rights. For a quarter of a century the two movements, to free the slave and liberate the woman, nourished and strengthened one another." (*A Century of Struggle*, p. 159.)

The feminist crusade of the late 19th and early 20th

centuries was mainly a branch of that middle-class progressivism which tried to effect democratic reforms in the structure of American capitalism.

The socialist struggle against wage slavery is today's parallel to the abolitionist struggle against chattel slavery—and the current strivings for women's liberation bear a comparable relation to it. Marxists must be in the forefront of this movement, which is a component of the most progressive tendencies of our time, and vigorously participate in it with their program and ideas. Many of the most effective fighters for women's liberation will get their organizational training and political education within a revolutionary movement, such as that represented by the Socialist Workers Party and the Young Socialist Alliance.

The rebirth of interest in "the woman question" indicates that the vanguard of "the second sex" is beginning to swing into action along with the insurgent blacks and student rebels. They will be joined in turn and in time by re-aroused contingents of militant workers.

To be sure, these elements are still marching separately and at their own pace. The strategic task is to have them strike at the main enemy together. The unified struggle of all these forces against capitalist domination is the key to bringing about "a new birth of freedom" for both women and workers through a socialist America in a socialist world.

October 1969

WOMEN'S EMANCIPATION AND THE WORKING CLASS

Women in Cuba: The Making of a Revolution Within the Revolution
VILMA ESPÍN
ASELA DE LOS SANTOS
YOLANDA FERRER

The integration of women in the ranks and leadership of the Cuban Revolution was intertwined with the proletarian course led by Fidel Castro from the start. This is the story of that revolution and how it transformed the women and men who made it. $17. Also in Spanish, Farsi, Greek.

The Origin of the Family, Private Property, and the State
FREDERICK ENGELS

The emergence of class-divided society gave rise to repressive state bodies and the oppression of women to enable the ruling classes to pass along wealth and privilege. Engels discusses the consequences for working people of these class institutions—from their ancient forms to their modern versions. $15. Also in Spanish and Farsi.

Women's Liberation and the African Freedom Struggle
THOMAS SANKARA

"There is no true social revolution without the liberation of women," explains the leader of the 1983–87 revolution in the West African country of Burkina Faso. $5. Also in Spanish, French, Farsi, Arabic.

CUBA'S SOCIALIST REVOLUTION

New!
Revolution and the Road to Peace in Colombia
The Example of the Cuban Revolution
FIDEL CASTRO

"No crime can be committed in the name of revolution," Fidel Castro declares, drawing from the example set by working people of Cuba as they took state power out of the hands of its capitalist rulers. In 2008, as part of efforts to end six decades of armed conflict in Colombia, he shared the exemplary record of Cuba's revolutionary struggle with the Revolutionary Armed Forces of Colombia (FARC) and the world. $10. Also in Spanish and French.

Che Guevara on Economics and Politics in the Transition to Socialism
CARLOS TABLADA

It's essential for working people to win state power, said Ernesto Che Guevara. "Then there's the second stage, maybe more difficult than the first"—the transition from dog-eat-dog capitalism to socialism. Includes Fidel Castro's 1987 speech "Che's Ideas Are Absolutely Relevant Today." New edition with substantially expanded selections from Guevara's writings. $17. Also in Spanish.

Cuba and Angola
Fighting for Africa's Freedom and Our Own
FIDEL CASTRO, RAÚL CASTRO, NELSON MANDELA

In March 1988, the army of South Africa's apartheid regime was dealt a crushing defeat by Cuban, Angolan, and Namibian combatants in Angola. Here leaders and participants tell the story of the 16-year-long internationalist mission that strengthened the Cuban Revolution as well. $12. Also in Spanish.

PATHFINDERPRESS.COM

FROM PATHFINDER

The Fight Against Jew-Hatred and Pogroms in the Imperialist Epoch
Stakes for the International Working Class

V.I. LENIN, LEON TROTSKY
FARRELL DOBBS, JAMES P. CANNON
JACK BARNES, DAVE PRINCE

Jew-hatred and pogroms—such as Hamas carried out on October 7, 2023—are part of the social convulsions and wars of the imperialist epoch. The authors explain why fighting Jew-hatred is decisive to the working class and oppressed nations of the world—and *what is to be done to end it*. $10. Also in Spanish, French, Greek.

The Low Point of Labor Resistance Is Behind Us
The Socialist Workers Party Looks Forward

JACK BARNES, MARY-ALICE WATERS
STEVE CLARK

The global order imposed by Washington is shattering. A long retreat by the working class and unions has come to an end. The bosses and their government are stepping up attacks on our wages, conditions, and constitutional rights. This book highlights opportunities for building a mass proletarian party able to lead the struggle to end capitalist rule, opening a socialist future for humanity. $10. Also in Spanish, French, Greek.

FBI on Trial
The Victory in the Socialist Workers Party Suit Against Government Spying

MARGARET JAYKO

The record of a historic victory in the fight for political rights, including the 1986 federal court ruling against government spying and excerpts from trial testimony by SWP leaders Farrell Dobbs and Jack Barnes. $17

The Teamster Series

FARRELL DOBBS

Four books on the 1930s strikes, organizing drives, and political campaigns that transformed the Teamsters into a militant industrial union movement. Written by the organizer of these battles and leader of the Socialist Workers Party. A tool for workers seeking to use union power and advance the fight for a party of labor. $16 each, series $50. Also in Spanish. *Teamster Rebellion* is also available in French, Farsi, Greek.

The Turn to Industry
Forging a Proletarian Party
JACK BARNES

A book about the working-class program, composition, and course of the only kind of party in the imperialist epoch worthy of the name "revolutionary." A party that can recognize the most revolutionary fact of this epoch—the worth of working people, and our capacity to change society when we organize and act to win power from the capitalist class. $15. Also in Spanish, French, Farsi, Greek.

Are They Rich Because They're Smart?
Class, Privilege, and Learning Under Capitalism
JACK BARNES

In battles forced on us by the capitalists, workers will begin to transform our attitudes toward life, work, and each other. We'll discover our worth, denied by the rulers and upper middle classes who insist they're rich because they're smart. We'll learn in struggle what we're capable of becoming. $10. Also in Spanish, French, Farsi, Arabic, Greek.

PATHFINDERPRESS.COM

EXPAND YOUR REVOLUTIONARY LIBRARY

Opening Guns of World War III: Washington's Assault on Iraq
JACK BARNES

The murderous assault on Iraq in 1990–91 heralded increasingly sharp conflicts among imperialist powers, growing instability of capitalism, and more wars. Also includes:

1945: When US Troops Said 'No!' by Mary-Alice Waters
Lessons from the Iran-Iraq War by Samad Sharif

In *New International* no. 7. $14. Also in Spanish, French, Farsi.

Cuba and the Coming American Revolution
JACK BARNES

This is a book about the example set by the Cuban people that socialist revolution is not only necessary—it can be made. A book about the struggles of workers and other exploited producers in the imperialist heartland, and the youth attracted to them. About the class struggle in the US, where the revolutionary capacities of working people are as utterly discounted by the ruling powers as were those of the Cuban toilers. $10. Also in Spanish, French, Farsi.

Labor, Nature, and the Evolution of Humanity
The Long View of History

FREDERICK ENGELS, KARL MARX
GEORGE NOVACK, MARY-ALICE WATERS

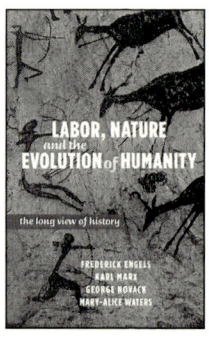

Without understanding that social labor, transforming nature, has driven humanity's evolution for millions of years, working people are unable to see beyond the capitalist epoch of class exploitation that warps all human relations, ideas, and values. $12. Also in Spanish and French.

New!
Cuba and the Independence War in Guinea-Bissau and Cape Verde
The Fall of the Last Colonial Empire in Africa
VÍCTOR DREKE

In 1974–75 the people of two West African countries, Guinea-Bissau and Cape Verde, put an end to 500 years of Portuguese colonial exploitation. Led by a popular movement forged by Amílcar Cabral, their struggle triggered the collapse of Portugal's entire colonial empire and brought down the 40-year fascist dictatorship in Portugal itself. Víctor Dreke's firsthand account brings to life this decisive victory. $12. Also in Spanish.

Malcolm X Talks to Young People
"The young generation of whites, Blacks, browns, whatever else—you're living at a time of revolution," said Malcolm in 1964. "And I for one will join with anyone, I don't care what color you are, as long as you want to change this miserable condition that exists on this earth." Four talks and an interview in the last months of Malcolm's life. $12. Also in Spanish, French, Farsi, Greek.

Pathfinder Press **accessible e-books** for the blind, those with low vision, or other challenges reading print books

For a list of current accessible titles, go to: pathfinderpress.com/collections/books-for-the-blind.

Visit bookshare.org for information on how to sign up.

PATHFINDERPRESS.COM

PATHFINDER AROUND THE WORLD

UNITED STATES
(and Caribbean, Latin America, and East Asia)
> *Pathfinder Books, 306 W. 37th St., 13th Floor*
> *New York, NY 10018*

CANADA
> *Pathfinder Books, 7107 St. Denis, Suite 204*
> *Montreal, QC H2S 2S5*

UNITED KINGDOM
(and Europe, Africa, Middle East, and South Asia)
> *Pathfinder Books, 5 Norman Rd.*
> *Seven Sisters, London N15 4ND*

AUSTRALIA
(and New Zealand, Southeast Asia, and the Pacific)
> *Pathfinder Books, Suite 2, First floor, 275 George St.*
> *Liverpool, Sydney, NSW 2170*
> *Postal address: P.O. Box 73, Campsie, NSW 2194*

BUILD YOUR LIBRARY!
JOIN THE PATHFINDER READERS CLUB

$10 / YEAR
25% DISCOUNT ON ALL PATHFINDER TITLES
30% OFF BOOKS OF THE MONTH
Valid at pathfinderpress.com and local Pathfinder book centers

Go to: pathfinderpress.com/products/pathfinder-readers-club

Pathfinder
pathfinderpress.com